With best wishes

Colin

Chuckleverse

11

"Better by far you should forget and smile
Than you should remember and be sad."
Christina Rosetti

"To be wildly enthusiastic or deadly serious - both are wrong. Both pass.
One must keep ever present a sense of humour. It depends entirely on
yourself how much you see or hear or understand. But the sense of
humour I have found of use in every single occasion of my life."
Katherine Mansfield

Chuckleverse

by

Colin Campbell

WESTBURY BOOKS

Chuckleverse

Arkwright

The boss has given me an order
to take a crowd on board a
boat I have to build;
it should be well filled,
going by the latest indications
of double room reservations.
Bookings are flooding in.

Three hundred cubits in length
means there's to be constructive strength.
I think I'll go for
gopher
wood.

☺

Avarice

If a law was passed
that arthropods had to wear shoes
I'd lose
no time fulfilling a need
to satiate greed
being a cobbler
to the centipede.

Auction

She holds up her numbered card
having stroked the paws of cabriole legs,
checked for woodworm,
run a hand over a chiffonier,
a desirable chesterfield, a rocking chair.
Daunting competition with dealers,
notebooked, taciturn people
telephoning distant bidders.
She leaves empty-handed.
I ask if she enjoys these sessions.
Not
a lot
she says.

Basic Subject

I've rarely excelled in my old grammar school
With my mark of C Minus the norm.
Where most of the masters believe I'm a fool
And remain the prime dunce in the form.

Equations in algebra never work out;
My attempts make old Fothergill weep.
Insomnia threatens while changing about
Nagging "x"s and "y"s in my sleep.

My Science is shocking, and French below par.
"Your declensions make Latin a farce,"
Said a teacher one day, "I can see why you are
Firmly fixed at the foot of the class."

School drama society meets every week,
And it's here that I flourish and star.
In *Twelfth Night* my role as a droll Aguecheek
Was considered the finest so far.

They've planned *A Midsummer Night's Dream* for next year;
A revival it's hard to explain.
One curious reason I did overhear
Was they hoped I'd be Bottom again.

☺

A Shropshire Lass

(With apologies to A E H)

When I was one and twenty
I heard a prophet say
That Hammerstein and Rodgers
Would reach the heights one day.
"They'll write of *Oklahoma*,
Make *the sound of music* swell,
And then *climb every mountain*
To produce a *carousel*."

When I was two and twenty
He whispered without shame
That on *some enchanted evening*
There is nothing like a dame.
He smiled with smiles aplenty
As I cried, "*I can't say no!*"
So, at last, dear Dick and Oscar,
I have married *Mister Snow*.

😐

Burning Desire

Lotioned legions lying, lazing
on the beach in August days
under heaven's light that's blazing
close to Walton-on-the-Naze,
where the bright midsummer sun
paints a tan on everyone.

Harassed husbands hauling hampers
out of cars by Clacton Pier;
parasolled and sand-duned campers
shunning Saint Tropez this year.
Children shouting, laughing, splashing,
scampering or pebble dashing.

Scorching sunny seaside's swelter,
tarmac sizzles near the Grand;
swirling switchback, helter-skelter
vying with a sweating band
playing under beating sun
tunes from *Annie Get Your Gun.*

Promenading parents paying
for the well-placed striped deckchair.
Stoically and breathless saying
they are used to tropic air.
Soft drinks or beer glasses filling—
symptoms of their annual grilling.

Bodies brown beyond believing,
scarlet faces, blistered too.
Bronzed Adonises achieving
all they set themselves to do ...
finally inland retreating
to off-season's central heating

Where wild winter waits with warnings
of a suntan soon to go
on its bitter icy mornings
with a likelihood of snow.
Then warm dreams begin to fade
of days once eighty in the shade.

The Sloth

I hang around most days.
Not a bit like the camel,
I'm an edentate mammal
quite happy to laze
in tropical trees
at my ease.

I can study the sky
in my dilatory way,
ever content to stay.
Slowly moving, high,
with jungle beneath—
minus teeth.

All my movements are slow;
I've never been one to race,
going along at one pace
of adagio.
You can't "go to town"
upside down.

Sonnet on a Guiding Light

What can I write of you my glowing star
who showed the way when darkness seemed to fall?—
and nurtured languid expectations far
beyond my trite existence until all
the world became Elysium to me?
Then you, my gentle angel led me through
a labyrinth of paths to ecstasy,
where romance flourished and true passion grew.
And still today, two hearts as one delight
in unison or harmony replete
that we together heard upon that night
when silently you led me to my seat.
The Plaza changed to heaven when I met
my lovely flambeau-bearing usherette.

By Gum

(A Filler)

Having anaesthesia
makes life at the dentist's easier—
but what a mess
if our LDS
tried to make us dopier
while hiding his myopia!

9

Cashing in

My dear Jane,
great to see you again,
rolling back years
and stifling tears
of joy. Glad you approved
of the meal. I was moved
to think you still cared
and remembered those shared
days long ago.
The parties, the fun,
heady days in the sun
when the wine flowed free—
before it was "curtains" for me
with that financial blunder.
No wonder
I still call you dear.

☹

Moto Perpetuo

Ant-like crawling
stalling
overheating
hooting polluting
lane hopping cheating
cursing reversing
brow mopping stopping
light crashing dashing
voluble swearing
at pedestrians daring
to cross at crossings
and somehow surviving
rush hour driving.

☺

Nuisance Call

She said, "You may have heard of us."

Feeling slightly murderous
with wrath and indignation raising
doubts on modern double glazing—
my blood pressure was also rising
at this style of merchandising.
Still, of course, she didn't know
we're moving from the bungalow,
and in a fit of anger I
told a most atrocious lie.
Politely, as befits a gent,
I said, "We hope to buy a tent,
so it's useless to keep praising
benefits of double glazing."
She said one of their merged firms
could offer us exciting terms.
She'd get in touch sometime next year
about their range of camping gear.

Why didn't we elect to be
concealed by ex-directory?

The Elephant

I often think of far-off things
like waterholed dry river springs.
In Regents Park the memory brings
a shedded tear.

In size I am extremely large.
My trunk calls are devoid of charge.
I've mammoth tales about the Raj
in days gone by.

It's never said that I'm effete,
I've carried all the world's elite
with ornate howdah - that's my seat
upon my back.

Have pity for a creature whose
first choice in footwear means I choose
a size nineteen in hiking shoes.
Sole-destroying.

Cats

They soft-paw-slink under parked cars.
Eyes of ochre ever watchful,
sinews tensed for deadly pounce.
Adding up the week's conquests;
consulting a fledgling file.
Avoiding enemy territory
while scanning no-man's land
of the avenue's vacant plot.

Winter brings solace of pampering
by firesides.
Dark prowls are forgotten;
life becomes warm purr-fection.

Couplets

Ireland's William Butler Yeats
left us work that never dates.

The great Johann Sebastian Bach
saw light of day in Eisenach.

Australia's own Percy Grainger
was a very good arranger.

That Austrian composer, Haydn
has a name that rhymes with Dryden.

All I know of Penny King
is that she rhymes with anything.

Mythology

Young Aphrodite
must have been a bit flighty.
No lady behaves
after rising from waves
so boldly flirtatious.
Good gracious!

Crossword Anagrams

Bears can change a sabre, fibre can be brief,
A fool at times aloof, or a flea become a leaf.
A moat can be an atom, and china turned to chain,
An orchestra a carthorse while trains reveal a strain.

Streams forever masters, Norwich, NW choir,
Anthem turns the man, and his praise begets a spire.
Minute minuet can now be played in fourths, for thus,
Discordant death is hated - time runs out with terminus!

☺

Morning Call

There are times I think
I'm double-0-seven's drink.
When the alarm clock's unheard
I've been shaken but not stirred.

😐

Lines from Noël

You astonished with the pace
with which you wrote and made us heed
your talent in *This Year Of Grace*.
You entertained *This Happy Breed*
of men in passing *Cavalcade*
a singular prodigious feat
of writing lines that never fade.

You overcame the *Bitter Sweet*
taste of past success thereafter
in *The Vortex* unforgiving,
enjoying years of *Present Laughter*
in a grand *Design For Living*.
While feeling full of *London Pride*
your fresh *Blithe Spirit* lit the town—
although your *Fallen Angels* sighed,
Hay Fever never got them down...

Even now a thespian strives
to be engaged in *Private Lives*.

☺

Assignation

An ill-assorted pair
we must have seemed.
Who would have dreamed
of a donkey and me in debate
at the paddock gate?

Just when I felt the
conversation had died,
old Long Ears cried,
"Now, what's your views on the Creation
or Reincarnation?"

I didn't have a clue.
He roared and chaffed;
hee-hawed, then laughed,
"I suppose I could return one day
as the Vicar of Bray."

☺

Down In The Forest

The caravan stood in the driveway,
their hampers were stacked in the hall;
the Jones's were off for the weekend
to get away from it all.

They drove to a spot in the Forest
to camp where the parking was free,
a mile or two from New Milton,
in easy reach of the sea.

They hadn't expected the welcome
awaiting them later that day—
for who should be camping beside them
but those Higgins from two doors away.

A home from home somebody called it,
which didn't go down very well.
Their weekend of trouble-free heaven
was turned into troublesome hell.

They decided to leave the next morning,
with tempers as bitter as gall,
and made for the centre of London
to get away from it all!

Cruft's Dog Show

Walking with affected air,
    knowing cameras are there,
they step into the limelight
    of TV's big night.

Groomed for the test
    looking their best—
coiffeured, shampooed,
    catching the frenzied mood.

On parade,
    poised for the accolade,
awaiting adjudication,
    you sense their agitation.
The dogs are nervous as well.

Driving Lesson

He had the usual learner's fears.
Where's the clutch? How many gears?
Then the cost of indecision—
Panic at his first collision
As he heard the irate toot
before the bump against the boot.
He froze with face pale green and sickly.
How did he find "reverse" so quickly"?

Conscientious Objector

Humpty Dumpty heard Kitchener call,
"Come on, enlist, and hasten the fall
Of William the Kaiser" - words meant to enthral.
But pacifist Dumpty remained on his wall.

Heavenly Fantasy

A year ago I stole the sun
and nailed it to the garden shed,
though with a hectic day's work done
I had no thought of early bed.

Basking amid summer flowers
in a deckchair on the lawn,
turning brown through sleepless hours,
smirking at a puzzled dawn.

The problem was I needed night
to cool the everlasting day,
when suddenly to my delight
I solved it in a simple way.

You see, last month I stole the moon
and hid it by the kitchen door.
The next day in the afternoon,
a BBC news item bore

following the Greenwich pips,
a tale of lunar mystery.
How could there be this strange eclipse?
The only one who knew was me.

☺

The Bounder

He makes his money from rubber plantations,
putting it into investments and shares—
but little for us, his poorer relations,
never conversant with stock exchange "bears".

Always the same,
he's a bit of a miser,
keeping his cash for a far rainy day.
In financial dealings we know that there lies a
tale of deception that won't go away.

Close to KL there's his biggest plantation.
Staggering profits have just been announced.
He sent me a cheque which gave rise to elation—
made out of rubber, of course, it has bounced.

Topless

I hold Ruth closely in my arms.
She calls me "Chuck", a sobriquet.
I am a slave to all her charms
although we met but yesterday.
We stand nearby the top-deck rail;
this night decides our destiny.
I clutch my head to no avail,
my toupee falls into the sea.
She giggles and then pats my head,
this all-forgiving lovely Ruth,
who never shows a sign of dread
when faced with Nature's naked truth.

Falling From Grace

He faced his good parishioners
And preached about the Word.
He captured
And enraptured
Them as all true hearts were stirred.
He spoke of sin and swearing
With ecclesiastic style,
Then produced a fine example
When he tripped up in the aisle.

Last Movement

The bishop sidled quietly,
almost unnoticed
not wishing to disturb.
Going overboard
he pushed aside ethics.
Removed
      my
            last
                  pawn,
and delivered the coup de grâce.
            Checkmate.

Chauffeuse

She would set him down
at "The Rose and Crown".
Which made us all think
she drove him to drink.

:)

Kaleidoscope

They say I give black looks when cross;
Look blue if life has lost its gloss.
Turn envied-green when I can't match
A writer in his purple patch.
While others try hard to infer
That I'm a whited sepulchre.
They jeer, "Your cloud's not silver-lined!"
But I don't care, I'm colour-blind.

Lover's Plea

I recall the night you put
Your ten-stone weight upon my foot.
Just try and think, dear, how it feels
When stamped on by stiletto heels!
You, the girl of all my dreams
Who turned sweet nothings into screams.
It's hard to dance the "light fantastic"
Wearing hose of strong elastic.
Nonetheless for you I pine.

                    Your Loving Limping Valentine.

PS

I realise it's far too late—
But could you lose a little weight?

Looking Ahead

My New Year resolution?
    To support an institution
like a home for geriatric
    patients.
Might make it three, a hat trick
    of donations.
But some of my relations
    say that by December maybe
an institution could be supporting me.

☺

My Paradise Lost

Fair harbinger of warmer days
when iridaceous crocus pays
its welcome visit once again.
There's colour in the window box
around the vernal equinox,
while prim green-fingered neighbours deign
to offer praise and show delight
at such an overwhelming sight
of bulbs erupting in full bloom
beside the quasi Tudor frame
standing here before we came,
a feature of our living room.

While others wallow and immerse
this season in iambic verse,
no practicalities we spurn.
Although, spring-cleaning is a chore,
and has this male nostalgic for
the winter, and its quick return.
Such heresy is not received
with acclamation by her, peeved
by husband's words so rashly said.
On being suitably reproved
I find I'm quietly removed
to labour long in garden shed

where, banished on a day in Spring
I find it difficult to bring
much rationality to mind.
A young man's fancy so they say
will turn to love now any day.
But I'm to memories resigned
to youth's bright world once there for all
to take the primrose path and fall
head over heels in love, and tell
of blissful new-found ecstasy—
but sadly, between you and me
she's turning heaven into hell.

Cold shouldering's a chilling thing,
especially in the warmth of Spring.

The Rebel

He vilified the government on points of legislation,
And criticised white papers after swift examination.
They branded him a maverick who was set on revolution
When he blew the whistle on a well-established institution.

They called him an iconoclast, with motives cold and sinister,
As he incurred the wrath of a popular prime minister,
And once was "sent to Coventry" for swearing at The Speaker
Which left his status and his credibility the weaker.

Through all his parliamentary life his manner was conducive
To riling members opposite with language quite abusive.
When asked to withdraw statements he would steadfastly maintain
That what he said was true, and be abusive once again.

But that was long ago, for as a Hansard scribe records
He mellowed quite a bit when seated, ermined in the Lords.
And when he died they praised him as he joined the late elite—
And placed him on a pedestal not far from Downing Street.

Out Of Sight

I could see him on the "box" Tim said,
worth watching he led
me to believe.
My interest dropped to zero
as he was the eponymous hero
in *The Invisible Man*.
Well, it was fine
for Tim,
but I saw no sign
of him.

☺

Piano For Sale

Eighty-eight keys,
best of pedigrees.
I'm afraid
seldom played.
A gem among
pianos. Overstrung
like its owner.

Good tonal range,
would exchange
for wooden fife
as wife
prefers lighter music.

Queue Talk

He waited in the straggling queue
With club mates from the snooker hall
Where chances had been very few—
He hardly put a cue to ball.
One of those bleak, depressing days,
Black-clouded, windy, cold and wet,
With agonies on shaded baize,
A day he wanted to forget.

They waited for the bus to come
As arguments came to a head.
"You should have won hands down, by gum.
How did you miss that final red?"
Bright traffic lights across the square
Yo-yoed through this dismal scene.
He thought they looked right through him there,
That taunting red and mocking green.

The bus arrived, they squelched aboard,
He'd finished cueing for the day.
His safety play had been deplored
By those who queued another way.
Arriving home he made a drink
Then slowly climbed the stairs to bed—
Remembering that snide, "You'd think
anyone could beat old Fred."

He travelled to the land of dreams,
Kept winning tournaments at will,
As each opponent's best laid schemes
Failed to upset his all-round skill.
He potted like a demon when
He won the Challenge Snooker Cup.
The champagne flowed, they cheered him, then
The blasted Teasmade woke him up.

Wimbledon Heads

In SWI9 they turn as robots;
    regular metronomes
set at various tempi—
    andante or allegro for the singles,
con moto for the doubles.

Above the heads
    panama, jockey cap, handkerchief,
or last resorted newspaper.
    Wearers come to pay court to seeds
maturing through rounds.

Players, their rackets pressed
    endure the sporting press,
forthright for a rain-halting,
    foot-faulting fortnight.

Cream teas and aces served.

Robotic heads swivel
    at the deuce of a game,
and await final days of judgement
    with laddered umpires.

34

Waste

They're in a mess for a while,
moving into a quasi Tudor style
bungalow; a little gem they say.
The other day
they sent a "new address" card,
which I found hard
to believe. Why did they ever
think of me? I never
write to them.

☺

Conflict

The manic red-faced frenzied looks,
the lunge towards the jutting jaw
are chronicled in pocket books—
a true account of what they saw.
The bestial snarl and brandished fists,
the blackened eye and cut on cheek,
all adding to the pencilled lists
of soccer referees this week.

☺

Well Trained

From the City line emerge
in their escalated surge
clerks and typists homeward bound,
finishing the daily round
via London's Underground.

Goblins of this underworld,
papers and umbrellas furled,
swarm as bees about a hive,
watch the creeping train arrive,
soon to be the half-past five.

Some among this weary horde
scan the big departures board,
hoping they will catch a main
line express, and respite gain
on an inter-city train.

Ticket seasoned workers rush,
trying to avoid the crush.
Commuters and day trippers too
have a fleeting troll-like view
of battle stationed Waterloo.

☺

Sacrifice

I read the bits on the side
of the yoghurt carton:
Protein.
Gelatine.
I'd set my heart on
a big lunch.

Yoghurt was point one per cent,
virtually fat free.
I thought
that it ought
in time to make me
much slimmer.

I found it was likeable.
The paunch put up a fight.
But, eureka!
a week
ago I saw with delight
my feet again.

Short Break

I'll tell you the worst first
he said, you've got a burst
water main by the gate.
The going paying rate
is quite high.
I'll have to buy
piping.

You're the third one this week
to complain of a leak
all in the same crescent.
Catching at the present
I'd say, sir.
We can't defer
digging.

They dug a long deep trench
releasing green clay stench.
Don't worry sir, we'll cope,
there's a trickle of hope.
They worked fast,
and then at last—
WATER!

☺

Name Dropping

"First names should have a certain style," the old musician said,
"Now, wouldn't it be ludicrous if Beethoven was Fred?
Or Schubert known as Harry and Mendelssohn as Mike?
Imagine Brahms as Charlie, or Rachmaninoff as Spike!
Who'd want to hear an opera composed by Jack Puccini?
Or the Devil's Trill Sonata by someone called Sid Tartini?
Old Verdi's popularity would wane if he were Bill,
And Bizet as a Robert doesn't seem quite right, but still,
Composers in the future may find they are not encumbered
By first or even second names, but simply opus numbered."

40

Spirited Complaint

How we loathe this infiltration
When hordes tramp along our drive!
To this trust house of the nation,
"Open half-past ten till five."
West Gate Lodge becomes a turnstile,
Canvas tea bars spoil the view,
Littered picnics by the sundial,
And the never-ending queue.

This is where we haunt at leisure
On the Regent's corridor,
Dancing sarabanded measure
On the polished marble floor.
Panelled walls designed by Wyatt
We can glide through after dark,
Into nights of rural quiet
Haunting orangery and park.

Curse this annual mass invasion
Of the camera-clicking throng!
Laying siege to our persuasion—
Grockletide is six months long.
Teachers hug their clip-board rotas,
Schoolgirls crocodile away,
Lollipopped, with ribboned boaters
To return another day...

With the day excursions ended
Clamour fades upon the ear.
Guided tours at last suspended
Until April of next year.
When the tourists have departed
From the grounds by car or bus
We begin to feel light-hearted
Now they've left the Hall to us.

Speakers' Corner

They're preaching their soapbox religion
at weekends in sunshine and rain,
facing applause and derision
near the arch at the end of Park Lane.
Most of them zealous and pious and brave;
their platform they say is the Word.
Arguments ranging from petty to grave,
or stupid, facetious, absurd.
They're promising heaven and threatening hell
surrounded by omnibus din.
Expounding their theories each Sunday to spell
out their thoughts on original sin.
In spite of these fine words some of them may go
to the hell that they weekly deride...
Like the call from the bus stop, I'm certain you know
there'll be standing room only inside!

Three Clerihews

Mister E C Bentley
Evidently
Had very strong views
On writing clerihews.

The small gym makes it hard
For Jean in her leotard
To perform anything acrobatic
So she just remains static.

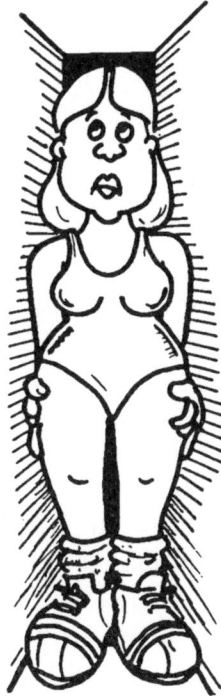

I'd wager a fiver
On Coventry's Lady Godiva
To win on any horse—
Riding bareback of course.

Operatic Clerihew

Why do some people cry
      Over *Madam Butterfly*?
Isn't it an opera
      About lepidoptera?

😐

Three Limericks

An eccentric old farmer of Wield
Put a wallaby into a field
Close to a sheepfold,
Now, lo and behold
Woolly jumpers are being revealed.

An explorer near here made frenetic
preparations, and was energetic
enough to attract
several sponsors in fact
to the North, which is always magnetic.

A light-hearted painter of murals
Did a wonderful scene of the Urals.
When a critic enquired
What made him inspired,
He said, "It's those singular plurals!"

🙂

Transient Amnesia

Walking through woods with their tall Surrey pines,
past "Danger Keep Out" of stern military signs,
I'm thinking of someone of whom I once read,
but her memorable name has gone out of my head.

This shocking forgetfulness causes alarms,
as I know that the poet was full of her charms
and wrote of her beauty with moving delight
after taking this girl to the golf club at night

to dance the late hours away on the floor,
knowing that she was the one to adore,
and drive her back home in a passionate haze—
a finale to one of the loveliest days.

Now, who was it ? Sarah? Penelope? Pearl?
I know that she was a John Betjeman girl.
At last, I've remembered, there was only one.
Of course! The delectable Joan Hunter Dunn!

Road Report

It's a terrible drive
On the M 25.
One big nightmare for everyone on it.
If it's hell that you seek,
Come along any week
And then circulate bonnet to bonnet.

This orbital wonder,
Or capital blunder
Was designed to make motoring faster.
Should you travel at speed
It may very well lead
To an anti or clockwise disaster.

People start changing lanes
Between Chertsey and Staines
To avoid the pre-rush hour hurry.
You can do just as well
Leaving this carousel
And drive off through the byways of Surrey.

Now, if news of this kind
Got around you might find
All the roads would become most confusing.
Being left high and dry
You would hear drivers sigh
For a motorway no-one is using!

The Warden

He came by a circuitous route,
not hurrying,
ignoring the hoot
from a passing driver.

He had the look of an official
making a point
in a judicial
inquiry concerning sleaze.

As he quietly approached he smiled,
"Good morning son,"
as if to a child,
"it's illegal to park here."

I was on the double yellow line
all right, and he
gave no hopeful sign
of a reprieve from justice.

"That's just the ticket," he said.

Cocktail Chatter

... he's always had this allergy
    my latest book is going well
some sort of celebrity
    stocks and shares are perfect hell
it's quite a simple modulus
    is that Gershwin's *Summertime*?
your theories seem so odd to us
    what's your views on modern crime?
avant garde is all the rage
    yes, a scotch and soda please
do you write the women's page?
    caught me just below the knees
my dear, it gave me such a fright
    he cultivates a charming lisp
what on earth's a troglodyte?
    can I press you to a crisp?
flying in from Tokyo
    yes, they say he's reading Law
honestly, I hate the show
    mother spoke to Bernard Shaw
how are things in Omaha?
    I think there's been a drop of rain
that's him standing at the bar
    nice to talk to you again
well, you know, it makes you think
    darling, I was quite bereft
will you have another drink?
    Oh dear me, there's nothing left!

☺

Zoology

Dinosaurs now long departed;
herbivorous things they were.
If creation was restarted
there's one breed I'd still prefer.

Thesauruses are extant creatures,
full of antonyms, and such
words that tax some donnish teachers
wanting to remain in touch
with modern idioms that yearly
find their way onto the page,
bearing definitions clearly
printed there for dunce or sage.

Latin phrases, words called abstract,
everything from A to Z.
Roget realised the one fact,
living language isn't dead.
Columned notes reveal the pleasure
he discovered in his quest
to produce fine books to treasure—
referentially the best.

Animals of old may perish,
lost in earth's antiquity.
The only one that I still cherish?
Thesaurus, he's the one for me!

☺

Immovable

The settlement was fixed at last
So we could go our separate ways.
I blotted out the happy past
Of pre-divorce Elysium days.

You left me the old Austin car
To drive away completely free.
I wasn't going very far—
You'd taken the ignition key.

☺

Prorogation

O rain! descend and kill the blight
Of loud exploding Guy Fawkes Night.
Dampen fires and receive
My gratitude, for I believe
It's frivolous, this annual show
To celebrate what years ago
Was nothing but a hare-brained plot
To remove that chambered lot.

Of course there are more subtle ways
Of closing parliament these days.

☹

A Twist In The Tale

I caused a stir,
well, is wasn't cordon bleu.
We had to put up with it;
all I wanted was a little bit
more.

They were aghast.
Old Bumble gave me a blast.
It was bloomin' awful gruel,
and the room service
was downright cruel
see?

They weren't to know
that as time went on I'd show
improvement from a poor start.
But fancy being staged by Lionel Bart!
Me!

Perversity

If doggerel is trivial verse
is catterel considered worse?
Of course its nothing of the sort
as both of them give paws for thort.

I've been inordinately rash—
this looks a bit like Ogden Nash.

☺

The Bricklayer

"I suppose you're on top of the world,"
I said, hoping
he would say yes.
"Not at all," he said;
"I guess
more like on top of the wall—
coping."

😐

Hope

We fell in love one summer
and wed one day in spring.
This Christmas I felt glummer
when you returned the ring.

There may be a solution—
a marital reprieve.
Why not make a resolution
and become my New Year's Eve?

☺

To Dick Francis

In racy style you write of horses
On those National Hunting courses,
Where "bent" trainers bribe their riders
To win Gold Cups on outsiders.
Or fall at important fences,
Knowing that the consequences
Blazed across the sporting page
Mirror depressed punters' rage.
Criminality is rife
In your equine-betting life.

But, as befits a thoroughbred
You're always that one jump ahead.

☹

Crossed Wires

Pa rebuked with angry words.
"Stop throwing pebbles at those birds.
or else I'll pack you off to bed!"
We had to stop once that was said.
I know we both were red of face,
more in anger than disgrace.
It put a damper on our day;
the rounded bullets thrown away ...
Though when thought back to childhood goes
I still hear Pa shout, "Stone the crows!"

Star Choice

Before the days of go-karting
We queued at the cinema
Not far
From the old town hall.
And like Lauren Bacall
Were ready to go Bogarting.

The Scorpion

I'm fond of crime-detecting prose
    where Holmes and Poirot never fail.
The books that I prefer are those
    that have that good sting in the tale!

☹

Shakespeare Erratum

I'm his greatest fan,
but when he wrote of
the seven ages of Man
from childhood to senility,
I'm sure that he must have known
few would condone
his omission of mortgage.

☺

Pardon?

An eye-catching board on two posts
boasts a good position.
Yes, sited well,
but, Oh Hell!
in my condition,
going to the theatre
I don't feel any better.
Seen as a short sentence
by the hospital entrance...
it's quite debilitating,
"Guard Dogs Operating".

☺ ☺ ☹